Beyond
Base Ten

a mathematics unit for high-ability learners in grades 3–6

Beyond
Base Ten

The College of William and Mary
School of Education
Center for Gifted Education
P.O. Box 8795
Williamsburg, VA 23187

Center for Gifted Education Staff, Second Edition:
Executive Director: Dr. Joyce VanTassel-Baska
Director: Dr. Elissa F. Brown
Curriculum Director: Dr. Kimberley L. Chandler
Curriculum Writer: Dana T. Johnson
Unit Reviewer: Dr. Susan G. Assouline
Research Assistant: Mandy L. Fordham

Edited by Jennifer Robins
Production Design by Marjorie Parker

ISBN-13: 978-1-59363-329-5
ISBN-10: 1-59363-329-7

Prufrock Press Inc.
P.O. Box 8813
Waco, TX 76714-8813
Phone: (800) 998-2208
Fax: (800) 240-0333
http://www.prufrock.com

Contents

Part I: Introduction

Introduction to the Unit

Unit Introduction: *Beyond Base Ten* investigates the concept of place value and the representation of numbers by using place value and non-place-value systems. Number bases other than Base Ten will be featured, especially through historical contexts of early civilizations that developed number systems that are different from the one we use today.

Unit Rationale: Place value is a fundamental and powerful concept that is the foundation for the number system used by all cultures today. Typical curriculum materials address this concept in a rote method. This unit goes beyond this by:

- analyzing the structure of our number system and other systems;
- examining the historical foundations of place value systems (Babylonian and Mayan) and non-place-value systems (Roman and Greek) over thousands of years in different civilizations;
- analyzing why Base Ten is the surviving number system; and
- presenting applications of other number bases in areas such as computers and electricity.

Differentiation for Gifted Learners: This unit gives students a much broader and deeper experience with place value using number bases other than Base Ten. This is challenging because it requires a deep understanding of the mathematical concept of place value, rather than just a familiarity with one system or the memorization of the values of the places in Base Ten without an understanding of the structure of the system. Reasons to use this unit with gifted learners include the following:

- The regular school curriculum generally does not probe place value and numeral concepts other than Base Ten. This unit provides those additional experiences.
- Number operations done in a base other than Base Ten require a much deeper understanding of the algorithms and require serious thinking.
- The study of number systems other than Base Ten is analogous to understanding the structure of one's native language by studying a foreign language.
- The unit also includes some enriching experiences in applications of number bases, problem solving, and history of mathematics. These are appropriate for all students but are especially well suited for students who are mathematically adept because they are more likely to take advanced coursework.
- Roman numerals are not included in National Council of Teachers of Mathematics (NCTM) standards, but they are useful for students to know because they are still used in numbering prefaces and chapters, on watch faces, to give dates on old films, and the like. Remember that NCTM standards are not a ceiling; gifted students can and should go beyond what is stated as curriculum for all students.
- Higher level questions are included throughout the unit.
- Writing is required beyond just giving numerical answers to questions and this requires more cognition. These activities will reinforce language arts standards.
- The task demands are more strenuous than in other curriculum materials. Students sometimes are asked to complete tasks with less teacher support than would be given in a typical math class.

- There is a large amount of mathematical content included in this unit that is covered in an accelerated time frame.
- Examination of number systems from different historical cultures requires analysis, a higher level thinking skill.
- Substantive extensions are suggested for students who want to investigate a concept further. These often require independent work and there is room for creativity in completing them.
- Much of the work in this unit is inquiry-based. Although this approach may benefit all students, inquiry lessons are a good approach to unleash the thinking abilities of gifted students.
- Appropriate problem-solving challenges are posed for mathematically gifted students.

Even a full treatment of all lesson extensions might not be sufficiently challenging for most highly gifted students. However, these students will benefit from this unit if they experience it at an earlier age than most other students.

Links to NCTM Standards: Place value is addressed in the Number and Operations Standard in grades K–5. However, this unit also is very appropriate for middle school students due to the depth and complexity of the way the concepts are addressed. Standards include the following for grades 3–5, "Students should understand the place-value structure of the Base Ten number system and be able to represent and compare whole numbers and decimals." This unit not only will address Base Ten, but will require students to understand representations of the same number in different bases and perform operations within other number bases.

Suggested Grade Level Range: 3–6

Prerequisite Knowledge: Students should have the following background knowledge prior to beginning this unit:
- Students should be familiar with Base Ten. Lesson 2 refreshes the basic principles, but it should not be the first time students have talked about place value.
- Students should be proficient in whole number operations of addition, subtraction, multiplication, and division.
- Students should understand the partial products method of multiplication. For example:

$$
\begin{array}{rrrr}
 & & 6 & 4 \\
\times & & 2 & 3 \\
\hline
 & & 1 & 2 & (3 \times 4) \\
 & 1 & 8 & 0 & (3 \times 60) \\
 & & 8 & 0 & (20 \times 4) \\
1 & 2 & 0 & 0 & (20 \times 60) \\
\hline
1 & 4 & 7 & 2 \\
\end{array}
$$

Length of Lessons: These lessons can be customized to an individual classroom by selecting or omitting various activities.

Timing: This unit can be completed as a 1–2-week experience or spread throughout the semester. It may be used in a pull-out or enrichment class. Not all lessons need to be included in the unit, and the order of lessons may be determined by the teacher. Table 1 gives suggestions for selecting lessons for various classroom needs.

Table 1

Suggested Lessons for Various Classroom Needs

Minimum Treatment of This Unit	Intermediate Treatment of This Unit	Maximum Treatment of This Unit
• Younger students • Limited time frame • Students who need more support	• Upper elementary students • Fewer than seven class periods available	• Middle school students • Upper elementary grades with at least eight class periods available • Students who are very capable
Lessons 2, 4, 6, and 8. Be selective about activities within the lessons. Adapt questions as needed.	Lessons 2, 4, 6, and 8. Select either Lesson 5 or 7. Do only the easier extensions.	All lessons and some extensions. Lesson 2 may be summarized as a quick introduction.
Align the pre- and postassessment questions to match what will be covered in the lessons selected.	Align the pre- and postassessment questions to match what will be covered in the lessons selected.	Do all assessment questions.

Extensions: Suggestions for extension activities are included within lessons and at the end of the unit. Some can be completed either individually or in groups. You might also keep a piece of poster paper hanging in your classroom and encourage students to generate questions regarding material they want to know more about; individuals or groups can be asked to find out the answers to these questions and report back as additional extensions. The extensions often require students to function somewhat independently. However, you may choose to assign extensions to less able students by writing a more scaffolded version of the task.

Assessment

Each lesson has suggested assessments but teachers will find many more ways to determine student understanding.

Journals: If students maintain a math journal, they can be asked to solve a single problem in their journal and explain their reasoning. A good technique to create an audience for student writing is to suggest that they write a postcard to a friend who has asked for help in solving the problem.

Preassessment: This is not a readiness test; however, it assumes that students know about Base Ten concepts and operations. It is intended to give you a baseline indicator of what students know before they start the unit. Typically, they should not do well on the preassessment. If some students do perform well on the preassessment, you should use the lesson and unit extensions to extend their learning.

Postassessment: This is included at the end of the unit. It is parallel in structure to the preassessment. If you administer both instruments, you will be able to tell if students learned the concepts as a result of participating in this unit.

Unit Glossary

Binary number system: Base Two.

Decimal number system: Base Ten.

Decimal point: The symbol that separates whole numbers from fractional parts in a Base Ten numeral. In the United States, a period is used to designate the decimal point, but in other countries, it might be a comma or another symbol.

Digit: One of 10 Hindu-Arabic numerals: 0, 1, 2, 3, 4, 5, 6, 7, 8, and 9.

Googol: The name given to the number resulting from taking 10 to the 100th power.

Logarithm: The power to which a base must be raised to get a certain number. If $a^x = y$, then the logarithm of y in base a is x. We can write $\log_a y = x$.

Number: The idea of how many of something exist.

Numeral: The written representation for a number of things.

Radix: The base of a system of numbers, such as *two* in the binary system and *ten* in the decimal system.

Radix point: The location in a number that separates the integral part from the fractional part. For example, in the decimal system, it is the decimal point.

Sexagesimal system: Base Sixty.

Vigesimal number system: Base Twenty.

Part II: Lesson Plans

Lesson Plans

Lesson 1: Preassessment

Instructional Purpose

- To assess student knowledge and understanding of unit topics

Materials and Handouts

- Preassessment (Handout 1A)
- Preassessment Answer Key (Teacher Resource 1)

Activities

1. Explain to students that they will be beginning a new unit of study focused on the representation of numbers by using place value and non-place-value systems. Tell students that in order to get a good sense of how much they already know and to be able to tell how much they have learned by the end of the unit, they will need to take a preassessment. Distribute the **Preassessment (Handout 1A)** and have students complete it individually.

2. Collect and score the preassessments using the **Preassessment Answer Key (Teacher Resource 1)**.

3. Have students discuss which aspects of the preassessment they found difficult. Explain that throughout the unit they will be thinking about challenging questions that relate to concepts on the preassessment.

Notes to Teacher

1. The preassessment given in this lesson serves multiple purposes. Performance on the preassessment should establish a baseline against which performance on the postassessment may be compared. In addition, teachers may use information obtained from preassessments to aid instructional planning, as strengths and areas for improvement among students become apparent.

2. Students should have a unit notebook and folder that they can use throughout the unit to respond to Math Journal questions and other written assignments, and to keep any handouts from the unit. The notebook also can hold a running list of unit vocabulary, which also should be displayed in the classroom in chart form.

Assessment

- Preassessment

Preassessment (Handout 1A)

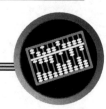

Directions: Do your best to answer the following questions.

1. What is the value of the digit **3** in each of these Base Ten numerals?

   a. 3,784 _____

   b. 204.316 _____

2. What is the value of the digit **4** in each of these Base Five numerals?

   a. 1432 _{Base Five} _____

   b. 2.4 _{Base Five} _____

3. Write 674 in Roman numerals. _____

4. Does the Roman system use place value? How do you know?

   _____

   _____

   _____

   _____

   _____

   _____

5. $123_{\text{Base Five}} = \underline{\hspace{2cm}}$ Base Ten

6. $19_{\text{Base Ten}} = \underline{\hspace{2cm}}$ Base Two

7. $24_{\text{Base Five}} = \underline{\hspace{2cm}}$ Base Two

8. What is the difference between the meanings of the terms *number* and *numeral*? Give examples.

    _____

    _____

    _____

9. Add these two numbers that are written in Base Eight notation.

$$
\begin{array}{r}
245_{\text{Base Eight}} \\
+\, 627_{\text{Base Eight}} \\
\hline
\text{Base Eight}
\end{array}
$$

10. How many symbols are needed to form a Base Twenty number system? _____ Explain your reasoning.

    _____

    _____

    _____

11. Complete the headings for this Base Sixty place value table. The units column has been done for you.

		ones (units)

Preassessment Scoring Guide
(Teacher Resource 1)

Directions: Do your best to answer the following questions.

1. What is the value of the digit **3** in each of these Base Ten numerals?

    a. 3,784   **3,000 or three thousand**

    b. 204.316   **³⁄₁₀ or three tenths**

2. What is the value of the digit **4** in each of these Base Five numerals?

    a. 1432 _{Base Five}   **100 or (4 × 25) or four twenty-fives**

    b. 2.4 _{Base Five}   **⁴⁄₅ or (4 × ⅕) or four fifths**

3. Write 674 in Roman numerals.   **DCLXXIV**

4. Does the Roman system use place value? How do you know?

    No, each symbol has the same value wherever it is placed; the placement of the symbol does not change its value.

5. 123 _{Base Five} = **38** _{Base Ten}

6. 19 _{Base Ten} = **10011** _{Base Two}

7. 24 _{Base Five} = **1110** _{Base Two}

8. What is the difference between the meanings of the terms *number* and *numeral*? Give examples.

    Number is the concept of "how many," whereas numeral is the written expression (notation) of the number. There are many ways (numerals) to write a number.

9. Add these two numbers that are written in Base Eight notation.

    245 Base Eight

    $+ 627$ Base Eight

    $\underline{1074}$ Base Eight

10. How many symbols are needed to form a Base Twenty number system?   **20**
    Explain your reasoning.

    You need one symbol for each number from 0–19. When you get a group of 20, you write 10, meaning "one group of 20 and no ones." The symbols can be reused by representing higher values when placed in a new position.

11. Complete the headings for this Base Sixty place value table. The units column has been done for you.

3,600s or (60 × 60) or 60^2	60s	ones (units)

Lesson 2: Introduction to Place Value

Instructional Purpose

- To establish understanding of place value in the Base Ten system
- To distinguish between the terms number and numeral

Materials and Handouts

- Base Ten Place Value Table (Handout 2A)
- Place Value Assessment (Handout 2B)
- 200 popsicle sticks per group
- Colored counters
- Rubber bands

Vocabulary

Digits: One of 10 Hindu-Arabic numerals: 0, 1, 2, 3, 4, 5, 6, 7, 8, and 9.
Number: The idea of how many of something exist.
Numeral: The written representation (symbol or mark) used to represent a number.

Activities

1. Discuss as a class the difference between a *number* and a *numeral*. Explain to students that a number is the idea of how many, and a numeral is the written expression of the number. Also mention that in everyday language we tend to use the word *number* for both meanings. Note that the numerals we use today are called *Hindu-Arabic numerals*.

2. Ask students how prehistoric humans counted (orally, mentally, or by writing). Explain that they probably used their 10 fingers to count and the system that evolved is called *Base Ten*.

3. Show students a concrete representation of the Base Ten system using the number 126 as an example. Show students how to sketch a place value table with cells large enough for students to place objects in them. Students will work in groups to represent 126 using a place value table and any of the following materials: popsicle sticks, colored counters, or rubber bands.

Hundreds	Tens	Ones

4. Have students count out 126 popsicle sticks (or the item your choose) and bundle every 10 sticks in a rubber band. Then have students create 100 by bundling 10 groups of 10 with a rubber band. Tell students to place the bundles in the appropriate cells on the place value table. Check student work (One bundle of 100, 2 bundles of 10, and 6 single sticks). Make sure that students understand that the popsicle stick model is a proportional model because each bundle is 10 times as big as the next smaller bundle.

5. Have students remove their popsicle sticks from the table. Explain to students that now they are going represent 126 using different materials (colored counters). Write the following key on the board that assigns values to colored counters.

> One yellow = 100
> One green = 10
> One blue = 1

6. Encourage students to represent 126 using the new color system. Check student work (one yellow, two greens, and six blues). Explain to students that other representations are possible (such as 12 greens and 6 blues). Prompt students to use the fewest counters possible to show 126 and require students to defend their solutions.

7. Discuss the advantages and disadvantages of using the colored counters and popsicle sticks to represent numbers. Explain that other representations can be used to show numbers as well. Use pennies, dimes, and dollars in the place value table to represent $3.24. Emphasize that the colored counter model is not a proportional representation because a dime is not 10 times as big as a penny. However, it is a valid, only different, kind of model for representing place value.

8. Explain to students that pictures can also be used to represent numbers. Have students sketch items in the place value table to demonstrate 126. Encourage students to sketch popsicle sticks or colored counters first and then their own original symbols.

9. Discuss with students how people have developed symbols to represent numbers over time. Explain that in Base Ten we use the symbols or numerals 0, 1, 2, 3, 4, 5, 6, 7, 8, and 9 to represent numbers. Ask students why these numerals are called digits and make the connection between the Latin origin of the word *digitus*, meaning finger or toe. Tell students that instead of drawing the pictures or using popsicle sticks, we can write 1, 2, and 6 in the table. Discuss as a class the meaning of each of these digits and why we don't draw a table every time we write a numeral.

10. Use the following questions to help guide the discussion further:
    - Are all digits numerals? (Yes)
    - Are all numerals digits? (No)
    - Which is larger: 246 or 462? Explain. (462, because the 4 in the hundreds place has more value than a 2 in the hundreds place.)
    - Why do you think we use the term *place value* to describe the system we use to write our numbers? (Where the digit is placed determines the value of the digit; in other words, the place where the digit is makes a difference.)
    - Imagine that you are a private detective. You find a torn piece of paper that originally had an amount of money written on it. Now there is only a dollar sign followed by the digit 4 and then the rest of the paper is torn off. Does the 4 stand for $4? What other amounts are possible? Explain. (The 4 could also be $40–$49, $400–$499, or any other amount that begins with a 4.)
    - What does the digit 3 represent in 3,456? How do you know? (Three thousands. It is the fourth digit from the right in the Base Ten place value table.)

11. Distribute the **Place Value Table (Handout 2A)** and have students complete the remaining place values on the table. The answers are as follows:

100,000,000s or hundred millions	10,000,000s or ten millions	1,000,000s or millions	100,000s or hundred thousands	10,000s or ten thousands	1,000s or thousands	100s or hundreds	10s or tens	1s or units

12. Use the following sentence stems and question to help students further understand place value.
    - Ten thousand means ten groups of ____.
    - A thousand means ten groups of ____.
    - A hundred means ten groups of ____.
    - Ten means ten groups of ____.
    - Why do you think that we call our number system Base Ten? (The value of each column in the place value table is 10 times the value of the column to the right.)

13. Have students write 23,456 on the **Place Value Table (Handout 2A)** and discuss the value of each digit.

14. Extend the idea of place value to fractional parts. Start with money as an example and tell students that $1 is a unit. Use the following questions to guide student thinking:
    - What is the relationship between a dime and a dollar? (A dime is ⅒ of a dollar.)
    - What is the relationship between a penny and a dime? (A penny is ⅒ of a dime.)
    - What is the relationship between a penny and a dollar? (A penny is ⅟₁₀₀ of a dollar.)

15. Ask students how this fractional relationship can be represented in a place value table. Tell students that in the United States we use a decimal point, which is a period, to separate the whole numbers from the fractional parts. Explain that in other countries they use a comma to separate the whole numbers from the fractional parts of a numeral.

16. Have students complete the place value headings of the second **Place Value Table on Handout 2A**. The answer are as follows:

100,000s or hundred thousands	10,000s or ten thousands	1,000s or thousands	100s or hundreds	10s or tens	1s or units	$\frac{1}{10}$s or tenths	$\frac{1}{100}$s or hundredths	$\frac{1}{1000}$s or thousandths

17. Have students write these numbers on their tables and ask students to give the value of each digit.
    - 7.23 [(7 × 1) + (2 × $\frac{1}{10}$) + (3 × $\frac{1}{100}$)]
    - 98.034 [(9 × 10) + (8 × 1) +(3 × $\frac{1}{100}$) + (4 × $\frac{1}{1,000}$)]

18. Distribute the **Place Value Assessment (Handout 2B)** and have students work in groups of three to complete it. Encourage students to give feedback on each other's accuracy and clarity. Every student should answer two questions.

Math Journal

- What is the value of the digit 6 in 86,789? Explain.
- What is the value of the digit 4 in 76.42? Explain.

Notes to Teacher

1. Do as much or as little of this lesson as needed based upon the preassessment results. If students are already proficient in Base Ten representations, you may limit your treatment of this lesson to the discussion on *number* vs. *numeral*.

2. To learn more about the differences in other countries, search the Internet using *decimal separator* as a search term.

3. The Hindu-Arabic system uses symbols that can be traced to the Hindus around 200 BC. The Arabs learned the symbols from the Hindus and carried them to Spain, where they eventually replaced Roman numerals. *Digits* are Hindu-Arabic numerals 0 through 9. Numerals may use one or more digits to represent them. Figure 1 is a Venn diagram that describes the relationship of digits and numerals. The set of digits is a subset of the set of numerals.

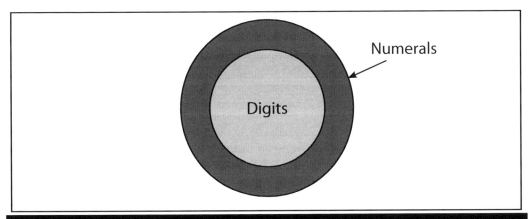

Figure 1. Venn diagram showing the relationship of digits and numerals.

Assessment

- Participation in class discussions and activities
- Place Value Assessment (Handout 2B)

Extensions

The following student activities can be used to extend the lesson.

1. Write everything you can think of about the number 12 in your math journal.

2. Find out about the history of Hindu-Arabic numerals and give a short report. Which system is older: Roman numerals or Hindu-Arabic numerals?

3. Who invented the symbol zero? Did the Romans have a symbol for the idea of zero?

4. Write the word names for *ten* in other languages. Are there any similarities?

5. Sometimes the Base Ten numeration system is called a *decimal system*. Look up the word *decimal* in a dictionary and figure out why this word describes Base Ten. Why do you think a decimal point is given that name?

6. Libraries sometimes catalogue books using the Dewey Decimal System. Find out why this system has the word decimal in it.

Place Value Table (Handout 2A)

	1s or units	
	10s or tens	

	1s or units •	

"Correct" Place Value Assessment (Handout 2B)

Directions: Roll a number cube or die to decide which question you need to answer on your turn. Then, follow the directions in the third column. Your teammates will check "Correct" if they think you responded correctly. They will check "Clear explanation" if your explanation made sense.

Problem	Numeral	Question	Teammates' Verification or Explanation
1.	23	Show what this numeral means with popsicle sticks. Explain.	❏ Correct model ❏ Clear explanation
2.	459	Show a model of what this means using colored chips. Explain.	❏ Correct model ❏ Clear explanation
3.	9,642	Use a place value table to explain what this numeral means.	❏ Correct table ❏ Clear explanation
4.	816	Choose one of the following to show what 816 means: popsicle sticks, colored chips, or a place value table. Explain.	❏ Correct model ❏ Clear explanation
5.	34,675	Explain which model would be better for showing the meaning of this numeral: popsicle sticks or colored chips.	❏ Correct answer ❏ Clear explanation
6.	$12.37	Draw a picture of the smallest number of bills and coins needed to show this amount of money. Explain why it is a Base Ten system.	❏ Correct picture ❏ Clear explanation

Lesson 3: Super Bowl XXXIX

Instructional Purpose

- To learn how the Roman Numeral system operates without using place value concepts

Materials and Handouts

- Roman Numerals (Handout 3A)
- Roman Numerals Chart (Handout 3B)
- Roman Numerals Chart Answer Key (Teacher Resource 1)
- More Roman Numerals (Handout 3C)
- More Roman Numerals Answer Key (Teacher Resource 2)
- Crossword Puzzle (Handout 3D)
- Crossword Puzzle Answer Key (Teacher Resource 3)

Activities

1. Read together **Roman Numerals (Handout 3A)** and discuss the rules of the system.

2. Distribute the **Roman Numerals Chart (Handout 3B)** and have students complete it. Discuss the students' answers as a class.

3. Start a discussion by asking, "Does the Roman numeral system use place value?" (Emphasize that it does not use place value because the symbols keep their value no matter where they are placed. Explain that position does not change the value of the symbol, therefore there is no place value. A nonexample is important in order to crystallize the concept and significance of place value.)

4. Ask students why they think the Roman system did not survive. (If they don't think of it, you might nudge them by writing this on the board: XVIII + CLIX = ? or "multiply VII by XV." From this they should see that computation is difficult without place value.)

5. Distribute **More Roman Numerals (Handout 3C)** and have students work in groups to complete it. Discuss their answers and thinking as a class.

6. Discuss why the symbol C was used by the Romans for 100 and why M was used for 1,000. Explain that C is the first letter of *centum*, the Latin word for 100, and M is the first letter of *mille*, the Latin word for 1,000.

7. Write "Super Bowl XXXIX" on the board. Use the following questions to guide a discussion.
   - In 2005, the Super Bowl was labeled in this way. What number is it? (39)
   - What is the Roman numeral that tells the number of the next Super Bowl? (XL)
   - What Super Bowl occurred in 2004? (XXXVIII, 38)

8. Distribute the **Crossword Puzzle (Handout 3D)** and have students complete it using Roman numerals instead of words.

Math Journal

Write the Roman numeral XCVII in your journal. Write a description of how you would explain this to a friend who did not know about Roman numerals. Ask three people older than you to figure out what number is represented. If a person does not know, explain how to interpret the symbols.

Note to Teacher

The early Romans used IIII for 4 and VIIII for 9. But, the system that has come down to us today uses the principle that a smaller number appearing before a larger means to subtract the smaller from the larger. So we use IV for four and IX for nine. However, it is common to see the four on a clock or watch given as IIII. If you can find it, there is an excellent article written by Kimberly Palmer on this topic in *The Wall Street Journal* on September 24, 2004, entitled "When the Big Hand Points to the IV, Some Get Ticked Off." It suggests that IIII is used to balance the VIII on the left side.

Extensions

The following student activities can be used to extend the lesson.

1. Here are two interesting questions. You might make your own conjecture about the reason. (If you find any evidence to explain why Roman Numerals are used this way, please send an e-mail with your findings to the author at dtjohn@wm.edu.)
   a. Find a book with a preface. What is a preface? Why do you think it is numbered in Roman Numerals? Why do you think the Roman Numerals are written in lower case letters?
   b. See if you can find out why Super Bowls and Olympic Games are numbered with Roman numerals.

2. Find some other examples of how Roman Numerals are used today.

Roman Numerals (Handout 3A)

There are variations on how some numbers are represented in this system but these are the most common rules used today.

1. Roman Numerals are written and read from left to right.

2. Symbols used are I, V, X, L, C, D, and M. (They usually are uppercase letters but lowercase are also used in modern times.)

    I = 1
    V = 5
    X = 10
    L = 50
    C = 100
    D = 500
    M = 1000

3. Numbers are represented by adding and subtracting.
    a. If numerals of equal value are placed side by side, they are added. I, X, and C may be used up to three times in a row. Examples:

        III = 3
        XX = 20
        CCC = 300

    b. When a smaller numeral appears before a larger numeral, the smaller is subtracted from the larger. Only certain cases of this are allowed: I is only placed before a V or X; X is only placed before L or C; C is only placed before D or M.

        IV = 4
        IX = 9
        XL = 40
        XC = 90
        CD = 400
        CM = 900

    c. Now that you know a symbol for 90 (XC) and a symbol for 9 (IX), you can write 99 in Roman Numerals by thinking "90 + 9": XCIX. (*Note:* The Romans did not write IC for 99. If you cannot sleep tonight until you find out why, see a guess about why found below under the symbol ♥.)

4. When writing a Roman Numeral, the largest number is written first, followed by numbers of equal or lesser value. Example: To write 2,349, think of 2,000 = MM, 300 = CCC, 40 = XL, and 9 = IX. So, 2,349 = MMCCCXLIX.

5. V, L, and D are not used in a row because when added, they total an existing numeral. VV = X, so X is used instead. Likewise, LL = C and DD = M, so the single symbol is used instead.

♥ Consider the list of symbols copied from (2) above. The symbols with an asterisk (*) in front can be subtracted from the next two symbols after it in the list. It looks like a pattern. Describe the pattern in your own words or mark the list in colored pencils.

*I = 1
V = 5
*X = 10
L = 50
*C = 100
D = 500
M = 1,000

If you stick with this pattern, you should not put I before C because they are too far away from each other in the list.

Speaking of patterns, what pattern do you notice here?

IV = 4
IX = 9
XL = 40
XC = 90
CD = 400
CM = 900

(That's what mathematics *is*, the study of patterns!)

Roman Numerals Chart (Handout 3B)

Hindu-Arabic Numeral	Roman Numeral	Hindu-Arabic Numeral	Roman Numeral
1	I	30	
2		36	
3		40	
4		48	
5	V	50	L
6		60	
7		64	
8		70	
9		79	
10	X	80	
11		88	
12		90	
13		99	
14		100	C
15		250	
16		450	
17		500	D
18		674	
19		1,000	M
20		1,284	

Roman Numerals Chart Answer Key (Teacher Resource 1)

Hindu-Arabic Numeral	Roman Numeral	Hindu-Arabic Numeral	Roman Numeral
1	I	30	XXX
2	II	36	XXXVI
3	III	40	XL
4	IV	48	XLVIII
5	V	50	L
6	VI	60	LX
7	VII	64	LXIV
8	VIII	70	LXX
9	IX	79	LXXIX
10	X	80	LXXX
11	XI	88	LXXXVIII
12	XII	90	XC
13	XIII	99	XCIX
14	XIV	100	C
15	XV	250	CCL
16	XVI	450	CDL
17	XVII	500	D
18	XVIII	674	DCLXXIV
19	XIX	1,000	M
20	XX	1,284	MCCLXXXIV

More Roman Numerals (Handout 3C)

1. Sometimes movies have the year of release written in Roman Numerals. What year was each of these movies made?

   a. *Rocky*:   MCMLXXVI   _____

   b. *Gone With the Wind*:   MCMXXXIX   _____

   c. *Ben-Hur:*   MCMLIX   _____

2. Write the following years in Roman Numerals:

   a. 1999   _____

   b. 2000   _____

   c. 2004   _____

3. International Olympic competitions are numbered with Roman Numerals.

   a. The 2004 Summer Olympics in Athens were designated as "XXVIII." What number is this?

   _____

   b. What will the Roman Numerals be for the 2008 Summer Olympics?

   _____

More Roman Numerals Answer Key (Teacher Resource 2)

1. Sometimes movies have the year of release written in Roman Numerals. What year was each of these movies made?

    a. *Rocky*:   MCMLXXVI   **1976**
    b. *Gone With the Wind*:   MCMXXXIX   **1939**
    c. *Ben-Hur*:   MCMLIX   **1959**

2. Write the following years in Roman Numerals:

    a. 1999   **MCMXCIX**
    b. 2000   **MM**
    c. 2004   **MMIV**

3. International Olympic competitions are numbered with Roman Numerals.

    a. The 2004 Summer Olympics in Athens were designated as "XXVIII." What number is this?   **28**
    b. What will the Roman Numerals be for the 2008 Summer Olympics?   **XXIX**

Crossword Puzzle (Handout 3D)

Directions: Write the Roman numeral for each clue.

Clues

Across	Down
1. 2712	2. 779
5. 227	3. 26
7. 2000	4. 3
8. 88	6. 73
9. 44	7. 1009
10. 99	

1:M	M	2:D	C	C	3:X	I	4:I	
		C			X		I	
5:C	C	X	X	V	I	I	I	
		L			I			
		X		6:L			7:M	M
8:L	X	X	X	V	I	I	I	
		I		X			X	
	9:X	L	I	V				
			I					
	10:X	C	I	X				

Lesson 4: Base Five

Instructional Purpose

- To discover another representation system for counting based on groupings by five (Base Five) rather than Base Ten

Materials and Handouts

- Base Five Place Value Table (Handout 4A)
- Base Five Chart (Handout 4B)
- Base Five Chart Answer Key (Teacher Resource 1)
- Exponents and Bases (Handout 4C)
- Base Five Assessment (Handout 4D)
- Base Five Assessment Answer Key (Teacher Resource 2)
- Extra for Experts! (Handout 4E)
- Extra for Experts! Answer Key (Teacher Resource 3)
- 200 popsicle sticks per group
- Rubber bands
- Pennies, nickels, and quarters (real, plastic, or paper)

Vocabulary

Radix: The base of a system of numbers, such as two in the binary system and ten in the decimal system.

Radix point: The location in a number that separates the integral part from the fractional part. For example, in the decimal system, it is the decimal point.

Activities

1. Imagine with students that the class travels to another planet, Planet Evifesab, where the inhabitants have only one hand with five fingers. Discuss with the students the differences that might exist in their system of counting. Introduce Base Five by helping students arrive at the conclusion that every group of five on the planet would get bundled or exchanged for one group of five. Then, every five groups of five become one group of 25, and so forth.

2. Display the **Base Five Place Value Table (Handout 4A)** on an overhead projector. Write the digits 2 and 3 in the two columns that are farthest to the right. Tell students that they are to assume that the inhabitants of Planet Evifesab use digits that are used on Earth. Ask students what 23 would mean in their system. Encourage students to think about this from multiple perspectives, including two groups of five and three left over.

3. Distribute the **Base Five Place Value Table (Handout 4A)** and have students determine the headings for the Planet Evifesab counting system. Have students explain their selected headings. Ask: "We call our customary number system 'Base Ten.' What do you think we should call this system?" (Base Five)

125s or one-hundred twenty-fives	25s or twenty-fives	5s or fives	1s or units

4. Distribute popsicle sticks and rubber bands to groups of students. Ask the groups to bundle them on the desktop using a Base Five grouping. For example, when they get a group of five, they need to rubber band the group. When they reach five bundles of five, they need to put them into another larger bundle. Have a representative from different groups demonstrate one of the following Base Ten numbers on the overhead projector.
   - 6
   - 37
   - 131

5. Discuss the difficulty of showing numbers with popsicle sticks and ask students for simpler ways to show a number in the Planet Evifesab system. Encourage students to think about writing numerals in the Place Value Table. Emphasize that the place value of each column is five times the value of the column to its right. Have students practice writing the digits in the **Base Five Place Value Table (Handout 4A)** for the numbers they represented with popsicle sticks above.
   ($6_{\text{Base Ten}} = 11_{\text{Base Five}}$, $37_{\text{Base Ten}} = 122_{\text{Base Five}}$, and $131_{\text{Base Ten}} = 1011_{\text{Base Five}}$)

6. Ask: "If we write the numeral 23, does it mean Base Ten or Base Five?" (Answer: If we do not give a subscript, we assume it means Base Ten. But, when any other number base is used, there must be a subscript to indicate the base.)

7. Ask: "What is the largest digit used in Base Five?" Emphasize that the answer is four because if you have five of something you do not record five; rather, you trade it in for one group of the value of the next column on the left. Connect this idea to the Base Ten system for students and note that we do not have a single symbol or digit for ten in Base Ten.

8. Distribute the **Base Five Chart (Handout 4B)** and have students complete it. Discuss student answers and their thinking.

9. Give students quarters, nickels, and pennies. Have them show how 97¢ would be represented using the smallest possible number of coins. Use the following questions to guide a class discussion.
   - How many of each coin did you use? (Three quarters, four nickels, and two pennies)
   - Why are pennies, nickels, and quarters good materials to represent Base Five counting methods? (Every time you have five of a coin of a lower value, you trade it for the higher value coin.)
   - In your opinion, are popsicle sticks or coins easier to show Base Five representation of numbers? Why?

10. Have students use coins to answer the following problems.
    - $97_{\text{Base Ten}} = $ _____ $_{\text{Base Five}}$ (342, the same number of coins used above to make 97¢)
    - $63_{\text{Base Ten}} = $ _____ $_{\text{Base Five}}$ (223)
    - $234_{\text{Base Five}} = $ _____ $_{\text{Base Ten}}$ (69)
    - $1234_{\text{Base Five}} = $ _____ $_{\text{Base Ten}}$ (194)
    - $712_{\text{Base Ten}} = $ _____ $_{\text{Base Five}}$ (10322)

11. Distribute **Exponents and Bases (Handout 4C)**. Explain to students that *five* is the base in the exponential expression and that the *base* is the factor. The exponent tells how many times the base is used as a factor. Have students return to the Base Five place value table they made in Handout 4A. They should write the exponential form above the column headings as shown below.

5^3	5^2	5^1	5^0

12. Challenge students to extend the Place Value Table to include fractional parts. Have students solve the following problems.
    - What would $24.3_{\text{Base Five}}$ mean? $[(2 \times 5) + (4 \times 1) + (3 \times \tfrac{1}{5})]$
    - What would $24.31_{\text{Base Five}}$ mean? $[(2 \times 5) + (4 \times 1) + (3 \times \tfrac{1}{5}) + (1 \times \tfrac{1}{25})]$

13. Investigate why it is awkward to call the point a decimal point because "deci" means *ten*. Explain to students that the term *decimal point* is used for Base Ten, and for other base systems the term *radix point* is used to mean the point that separates the whole numbers from the fractional parts of a number. Tell students that radix means the base of a system of numbers, such as five in the Base Five system and ten in the Base Ten system.

14. Have students extend the Place Value Table by completing the lower table in Handout 4A. Provide students with these practice problems:
    - $30.1_{\text{Base Five}}$ $[(3 \times 5) + (0 \times 1) + (1 \times \tfrac{1}{5})$ or $15 \tfrac{1}{5}$ or $15.2_{\text{Base Ten}}]$
    - $12.34_{\text{Base Five}}$ $[(1 \times 5) + (2 \times 1) + (3 \times \tfrac{1}{5}) + (4 \times \tfrac{1}{25})$ or $7 \tfrac{19}{25}$ or $7.76_{\text{Base Ten}}]$
    - $4.231_{\text{Base Five}}$ $[(4 \times 1) + (2 \times \tfrac{1}{5}) + (3 \times \tfrac{1}{25}) + (1 \times \tfrac{1}{125})$ or $4 \tfrac{66}{125}$ or $4.528_{\text{Base Ten}}]$

Notes to Teacher

1. It is very important to use the suggested concrete materials in order for students to understand different base systems and make connections. Even if your classroom is composed of homogeneously grouped high-ability students, there will be some learners who will benefit greatly from the experience of showing the concept with concrete materials.

2. When you change a Base Ten number into another number base, you might relate the process to using the largest coins to make change. The use of the coins in this lesson is useful in establishing this connection.

3. You might have students find out what *subscript* means. Subscripts are used a lot in mathematics, so it is a term that they will see again. *Superscript* is a related term that also should be investigated.

4. You may use subscripts "Base Five" or just "Five" on a Base Five numeral. It also is acceptable to use the digit "5" in a subscript position, but it is very easy to confuse it with the digits in the numeral.

5. Students may ask why $5^0 = 1$ (as this is not intuitively obvious). One explanation is to think about a pattern in which you divide by the base to move from one value to the one below it. Start with any power of 5, say 5^4 as shown below. Divide by 5 to get 5^3. Continue dividing by 5 until you get to $5^0 = 1$.

$$5^4 = 625$$
$$5^3 = 625 \div 5 = 125$$
$$5^2 = 125 \div 5 = 25$$
$$5^1 = 25 \div 5 = 5$$
$$5^0 = 5 \div 5 = 1$$

If you extend the pattern a few more steps you get:

$$5^{-1} = 1 \div 5 = \tfrac{1}{5}$$
$$5^{-2} = \tfrac{1}{5} \div 5 = \tfrac{1}{25}$$
$$5^{-3} = \tfrac{1}{25} \div 5 = \tfrac{1}{125}$$

Assessment

- Base Five Chart (Handout 4B)
- Base Five Assessment (Handout 4D)

Extensions

The following student activities can be used to extend the lesson.

1. Explore logarithms. The term *log* is short for logarithm and a log is an exponent. The problem **$\log_5 25 = 2$** means **$5^2 = 25$**. 5 is the base and 2 is the exponent. Challenge students to find the missing values.
   - $\log_5 125 = ?$ $(3; 5^3 = 125)$
   - $\log_5 ? = 1$ $(5; 5^1 = 5)$
   - $\log_? 625 = 4$ $(5; 5^4 = 625)$
   - $\log_{10} 100 = ?$ $(2; 10^2 = 100)$

2. Find out what a googol is and write this number in exponential notation. (Answer: 10^{100}; this is written as a 1 followed by 100 zeroes.)

3. Have students complete **Extra for Experts (Handout 4E)**. This activity asks students to add and subtract in Base Five. Computation in different number bases is the subject of Lesson 8.

4. Write 4922 $_{\text{Base Eight}}$ on the board and ask students what is wrong with this expression. (You cannot use the digit 9 in Base Eight. Even though you have not explicitly talked about Base Eight, students should be able to make this connection.)

Base Five Place Value Table (Handout 4A)

			Units

	Units			

Base Five Chart (Handout 4B)

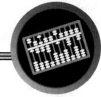

Directions: Write the following numbers as Base Five numerals. Some are done for you.

Base Ten Numeral	Base Five Numeral	Base Ten Numeral	Base Five Numeral
1	1	16	
2		17	
3		18	
4		19	
5		20	
6		21	
7		22	
8		23	
9		24	
10		25	
11		26	101
12		27	
13		28	
14	24	29	
15		30	

Base Five Chart Answer Key
(Teacher Resource 1)

Directions: Write the following numbers as Base Five numerals. Some are done for you.

Base Ten Numeral	Base Five Numeral	Base Ten Numeral	Base Five Numeral
1	1	16	31
2	2	17	32
3	3	18	33
4	4	19	34
5	10	20	40
6	11	21	41
7	12	22	42
8	13	23	43
9	14	24	44
10	20	25	100
11	21	26	101
12	22	27	102
13	23	28	103
14	24	29	104
15	30	30	110

Exponents and Bases (Handout 4C)

Base Five

$5^0 = 1$

$5^1 = 5$

$5^2 = 5 \times 5 = 25$

$5^3 = 5 \times 5 \times 5 = 125$

$5^4 = 5 \times 5 \times 5 \times 5 = 625$

$5^5 = ?$

Base Ten

$10^0 = 1$

$10^1 = 10$

$10^2 = 10 \times 10 = 100$

$10^3 = 10 \times 10 \times 10 = 1,000$

$10^4 = 10 \times 10 \times 10 \times 10 = 10,000$

$10^5 = ?$

Note: In the last example above, 10 is called the **base** and 5 is called the **exponent**.

Base Five Assessment (Handout 4D)

Directions: Fill in each blank. Show how you got your answer.

1. $42_{\text{Base Ten}}$ = _____ Base Five

2. $101_{\text{Base Ten}}$ = _____ Base Five

3. $42_{\text{Base Five}}$ = _____ Base Ten

4. $1002_{\text{Base Five}}$ = _____ Base Ten

5.   Give the value of each of the digits in this Base Five numeral: $32.14_{\text{Base Five}}$

_____

_____

_____

_____

_____

Base Five Assessment Answer Key (Teacher Resource 2)

Directions: Fill in each blank. Show how you got your answer.

1. $42_{\text{Base Ten}} = \underline{\mathbf{132}}\ _{\text{Base Five}}$

2. $101_{\text{Base Ten}} = \underline{\mathbf{401}}\ _{\text{Base Five}}$

3. $42_{\text{Base Five}} = \underline{\mathbf{22}}\ _{\text{Base Ten}}$

4. $1002_{\text{Base Five}} = \underline{\mathbf{127}}\ _{\text{Base Ten}}$

5.   Give the value of each of the digits in this Base Five numeral $32.14_{\text{Base Five}}$

   $\underline{\mathbf{(3 \times 5) + (2 \times 1) + (1 \times \frac{1}{5}) + (4 \times \frac{1}{25})}}$

Extra for Experts! (Handout 4E)

Directions: Can you add and subtract in Base Five? Try these problems and then convert the numbers to Base Ten to solve and check. An example is done for you.

Base Five Version of the Problem	Change to Base Ten
1. 34 +23 — 112	Check: 19 +13 — 32 Because 112 $_\text{Base Five}$ = 32 $_\text{Base Ten}$, it is likely that the answer in the first column is correct.
2. 22 +33	
3. 424 +412	
4. Subtract. Remember, this is Base Five! 43 −14	
5. 321 −123	

41

Extra for Experts! Answer Key
(Teacher Resource 3)

Directions: Can you add and subtract in Base Five? Try these problems and then convert the numbers to Base Ten to solve and check. An example is done for you.

Base Five Version of the Problem	Change to Base Ten
1. 34 +23 112	Check: 19 +13 32 Because 112 $_{Base\ Five}$ = 32 $_{Base\ Ten}$, it is likely that the answer in the first column is correct.
2. 22 +33 110	12 +18 30 Because 110 $_{Base\ Five}$ = 30 $_{Base\ Ten}$, it is likely that the answer in the first column is correct.
3. 424 +412 1341	114 +107 221 Because 1341 $_{Base\ Five}$ = 221 $_{Base\ Ten}$, it is likely that the answer in the first column is correct.
4. Subtract. Remember, this is Base Five! 43 −14 24	23 −9 14 Because 24 $_{Base\ Five}$ = 14 $_{Base\ Ten}$, it is likely that the answer in the first column is correct.
5. 321 −123 143	86 −38 48 Because 143 $_{Base\ Five}$ = 48 $_{Base\ Ten}$, it is likely that the answer in the first column is correct.

Lesson 5: Babylonians and Base Sixty

Instructional Purpose

- To explore another number system, Base Sixty, which was used by the Babylonian civilization

Materials and Handouts

- Babylonian Numerals (Handout 5A)
- Babylonian Practice (Handout 5B)
- Babylonian Practice Answer Key (Teacher Resource 1)
- Babylonian Table (Handout 5C)
- Babylonian Table Answer Key (Teacher Resource 2)
- Calculators for each group

Activities

1. Explain to students that early civilizations developed different number systems. Tell students that the Babylonian culture flourished in ancient times in the valley between the Tigris and Euphrates River in what is present-day Iraq. Have students locate the region on a map.

2. Tell students that the Babylonians used a number base of 60 that they developed about 4,000 years ago. Have students create a place value table for Base Sixty with at least four columns. It should look like this:

216,000's	3,600's	60's	1's

3. Use the following questions to lead a class discussion.
   - How many symbols would this system require? (Theoretically 60, but they did not have a zero so there were only 59.)
   - Why do you think this system would be easier or harder to work with compared to Base Ten or Base Five?

4. Distribute **Babylonian Numerals (Handout 5A)**. Have students work in groups and look for patterns in the table. Have the groups share their thinking in a class discussion. Use the following questions to help guide the discussion:
   - Suppose you had to describe to a friend over the phone how the symbols of this system are constructed. How would you explain the way the symbols are constructed?
   - Where is the zero? (The Babylonians did not have one!)
   - What could you use instead of a symbol for zero? (Leave a space. That is what the Babylonians did.)

5. Distribute **Babylonian Practice (Handout 5B)** and display a transparency of the handout on the overhead. Challenge students to change the Babylonian numerals into Hindu-Arabic numerals. Explain to students that commas can be used to

separate the numbers. For example, *12, 23, 42* means there are three columns in the place value table and the numbers stand for $(12 \times 3{,}600) + (23 \times 60) + (42 \times 1)$. Semicolons also can be used to separate the numbers instead of commas.

6. Discuss with students how the lack of a zero makes things confusing. For example, in the first item in Handout 5B, there is some ambiguity. Do the symbols mean $[(20 \times 60) + (5 \times 1)]$ or (25×1)? Tell students to assume there are no empty spaces in the second item on that page, but there is a space in Number 3 between the given symbols.

7. Have students work in groups to write the Babylonian numerals for the following Base Ten numerals.

   - 2   Answer:

   - 120   Answer:

   - 7200   Answer:

8. Discuss as a class how they all look the same. Reinforce the idea that without a zero, it is hard to distinguish the different numerals. The zero is very powerful in a place value system.

9. Distribute the **Babylonian Table (Handout 5C)** and complete the first one as a class example. Have students work in groups to complete the entire table. Tell students that there are no blank spaces between any of the symbols and they may use calculators. Remind students that there may be more than one answer for the Babylonian symbols and encourage them to record different possibilities.

10. Discuss as a class why Babylonians might have used Base Sixty. Explain to students that the Babylonians liked the fact that 60 is divisible by so many numbers and it made fractions easier. Have students list the factors of 60 (1, 2, 3, 4, 5, 6, 10, 12, 15, 20, 30, and 60). Point out to students that there are 365 days in a year and they made a calendar with 12 groups of 30 days each. At the end of the year, they added 5 days of holidays. Ask: "Can you think of another area where we use 60 as a base in measurements we make today?" (time: 60 seconds = 1 minute; 60 minutes = 1 hour; circles: there are 360 degrees in a circle.)

11. Have students extend their place value tables by adding more columns to the right of the units place. Have students fill in the values of three more places to the right of the radix point.

216,000's	3,600's	60's	1's or ones	$\dfrac{1}{60}$	$\dfrac{1}{3600}$	$\dfrac{1}{216{,}000}$

12. Have students identify the values of each digit in 123.456 $_{\text{Base Sixty.}}$
    [(1 × 216,000) + (2 × 3,600) + (3 × 1) + (4 × ⅟₆₀) + (5 × ⅟₃,₆₀₀) + (1 × ⅟₂₁₆,₀₀₀) or 223,203 $\frac{14,701}{216,000}$; it is difficult to convert this into a decimal representation (Base Ten) as there will be a repeating pattern of digits to the right of the decimal point and it does not start the repetition of a block of 3 digits until the 10th place to the right of the decimal point.]

Math Journal

- How can you tell if a Base Sixty numeral is odd or even?

Assessment

- Babylonian Table (Handout 5C)

Extensions

The following student activities can be used to extend the lesson.
1. Base Sixty is called a *sexagesimal system*. Look up *sexagesimal* in a dictionary and find the origin of the word.

2. Archaeologists have found clay tablets that recorded the Babylonian number system. The Plimpton 322, a famous clay tablet, is in the British Museum. Find out more about Plimpton 322 and share the information with the class. You can find a picture of the tablet on the Internet by doing a search for "Plimpton 322."

3. If the sexagesimal number 3, 8, 21 is written as a Base Ten numeral, what is the units digit? Explain. (1 because all values in all columns except the right column are multiples of 10 [60 is 6 × 10], so the units digit of the Base Ten numeral is only affected by the units column of the Base Sixty number. In this case, because there are 21 units in the Base Sixty form, you bundle two groups of 10 and leave the one.)

4. Write a computer or graphing calculator program to change a Base Sixty numeral into a Base Ten numeral.

Babylonian Numerals (Handout 5A)

Directions: Study the table and look for patterns.

1	11	21	31	41	51
2	12	22	32	42	52
3	13	23	33	43	53
4	14	24	34	44	54
5	15	25	35	45	55
6	16	26	36	46	56
7	17	27	37	47	57
8	18	28	38	48	58
9	19	29	39	49	59
10	20	30	40	50	

Babylonian Practice (Handout 5B)

Directions: Convert the Babylonian numerals to numerals in our system.

1.

Answer: _____

(Hint: This is only one symbol.)

2.

Answer: _____

(Hint: This is two symbols.)

3.

Answer: _____

(Hint: There is a space in between these two symbols.)

Babylonian Practice Answer Key (Teacher Resource 1)

Directions: Convert the Babylonian numerals to numerals in our system.

1.

Answer: <u>25</u>

2.

Answer: <u>2, 27 or (2 × 60) + (27 × 1) = 147</u>

3.

Answer: <u>6, 0, 9 or (6 × 3,600) + (0 × 60) + (9 × 1) = 21,609</u>

(Hint: There is a space in between the two symbols.)

Babylonian Table (Handout 5C)

Babylonian	Base Sixty (Using Hindu-Arabic Notation)	Base Ten Value
𒐖𒐕 𒐏𒐖 𒐖𒐖𒐖 𒑖	2, 23, 4	$(2 \times 3{,}600) + (23 \times 60) + (4 \times 1) = 8{,}584$
	3, 9, 25	
		10,000
𒐏𒐖 𒑖𒑖𒑖 𒐏𒑖		
	6, 31, 7	
		1,249
𒐏𒑖𒑖 𒐏𒐖 𒐕		

Babylonian Table Answer Key
(Teacher Resource 2)

Babylonian	Base Sixty (Using Hindu-Arabic Notation)	Base Ten Value
	2, 23, 4	$(2 \times 3{,}600) + (23 \times 60) + (4 \times 1) = 8{,}584$
	3, 9, 25	$(3 \times 3{,}600) + (9 \times 60) + (25 \times 1) = 11{,}365$
	2, 46, 40	10,000
	20, 6, 15	$(20 \times 3{,}600) + (6 \times 60) + (15 \times 1) = 72{,}375$
	6, 31, 7	$(6 \times 3{,}600) + (31 \times 60) + (7 \times 1) = 23{,}467$
	20, 49	$(20 \times 60) + (49 \times 1) = 1{,}249$
	15, 41	$(15 \times 60) + (41 \times 1) = 941$

Lesson 6: Base Two

Instructional Purpose

- To learn about the Base Two numeration system and some of its applications

Materials and Handouts

- Base Two Place Value Table (Handout 6A)
- Base Two Table (Handout 6B)
- Base Two Table Answer Key (Teacher Resource 1)
- Base Two Problems (Handout 6C)
- Base Two Problems Answer Key (Teacher Resource 2)
- Birthday Trick (Teacher Resource 3)
- Extending the Base Two Table to Fractional Parts (Handout 6D)
- Extending the Base Two Table Answer Key (Teacher Resource 4)
- Extra for Experts! (Handout 6E)
- Extra for Experts! Answer Key (Teacher Resource 5)
- 40 counters, tiles, or beans per group

Vocabulary

Binary number system: Base Two

Activities

1. Tell students that they will now be investigating a Base Two place value system. Distribute the **Base Two Place Value Table (Handout 6A)** and have students complete the headings.

32s	16s	8s	4s	2s	1s

2. Use the following questions to lead a class discussion.
    - What is the highest number you can represent on this table? (31)
    - If you added one more column to the left on the table, how many Base Ten numbers could you represent using this table? (Base Ten numerals 1 through 63)
    - If you write the headings of the table using exponents, what would they be? (2^4, 2^3, 2^2, 2^1, and 2^0)

3. Use a transparency of the **Base Two Place Value Table (Handout 6A)** and fill in the following digits for Base Two: 100111. Have students figure out what Base Ten numeral it is ($32 + 0 + 0 + 4 + 2 + 1 = 39$).

4. Distribute counters to groups and have students use them to show how various numbers of counters would be represented in Base Two. Show three on the overhead projector by putting one counter in the units column and then adding a second one to the units column. Trade those two for one counter in the twos column and add one more in the units column. The end result is one counter in the twos column and one counter in the ones column (00011). Try more examples and then ask students to try some in their groups.

5. Distribute the **Base Two Table (Handout 6B)** and have students complete it in small groups. Use the following questions to lead a class discussion.
   - What patterns do you notice in the table?
   - What are the advantages and disadvantages of using Base Two compared to Base Ten?

6. Distribute **Base Two Problems (Handout 6C)** and have students complete the problems.

7. Do the **Birthday Trick (Teacher Resource 3)** over the course of several days. If a student thinks he or she knows the trick, let him or her be the Guesser for another student; do not let the student reveal the secret of the trick. Once students see the trick part of knowing the answer, challenge them to figure out why the trick works. (Each card corresponds to a column from the Base Two place value table. The value of the column is the number at the top. So, a number only appears on cards where its binary numeral has 1's in those columns. Example: $6 = 110_{\text{Base Two}}$. So, 6 appears on the cards that start with 4 and 2.)

8. Have students work in groups to answer the following questions. Discuss their answers as a whole class.
   - What number(s) are on all of the cards?
   - What numbers are on only one card?
   - What other patterns do you notice on the cards?

9. Extend the Base Two table to include fractional parts. Have students complete **Extra For Experts! (Handout 6D)** after you work out the table in Handout 6A as a whole class.

Math Journal

- Look up the word *binary* in the dictionary. Write about why this word describes the Base Two number system.

Assessment

- Participation in class discussions
- Base Two Table (Handout 6B)
- Base Two Problems (Handout 6C)

Extensions

The following student activities can be used to extend the lesson.

1. If you can find a binary clock, set it up in the classroom before your place value unit starts and let the students observe it. At the end of the unit, have students explain what they have figured out about the clock. You may purchase a binary clock at http://www.thinkgeek.com. The clock is based on the binary number system. Six digits are used to indicate time. For example, 11:24:35 means 11:24 a.m. and 35 seconds. The clock uses 6 columns of small circular lights, each of which can be on or off. Each column represents a digit from 0 to 9. The two columns on the left indicate hours, the middle two are minutes, and the right two are seconds. The value of each column is determined by which lights are on. The bottom light, if on, is worth "1." The one above it is worth "2," the third one from the bottom is worth "4" and the top one is worth "8." Add the values of the light positions to get the final value of each digit.

2. Make a Binary Piano by going to http://homepages.strath.ac.uk/~cjbs17/ computing/resources/Binary%20Piano.doc. This is a paper model that illustrates the on/off nature of the Base Two number system by flipping tabs up and down on a paper keyboard.

3. Go to http://www.learner.org/channel/courses/learningmath/number/session3/ part_a/base.html for a discussion of Base Two in electrical circuits. The two digits of the binary system, 1 and 0, correspond to the presence or absence of electric current. Have interested students find out more and report to the class.

4. Introduce the fact that computers use binary forms of numbers. A computer is ultimately a two-state machine (e.g., the current in a circuit may be either on or off, an electrical gate may be open or closed). Have interested students find out more and report to the class.

5. Invite a speaker to talk to students about how Base Two is applied in computer science.

6. Have students complete **Extra for Experts! (Handout 6E)**.

7. Discuss this question: If you start with a Base Two numeral with a fractional part, will the Base Ten equivalent give a terminating decimal (i.e., no repeating cycle to the right of the decimal point)?

8. After students learn the secret of why the Birthday Trick works, challenge them to write an explanation of this in their math journals.

Base Two Place Value Table (Handout 6A)

					Units

Base Two Table (Handout 6B)

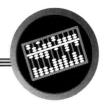

Directions: Write these Base Ten numerals in Base Two notation.
Some examples have been provided for you.

Base Ten Numerals	Base Two Numerals	Base Ten Numerals	Base Two Numerals
1	1	26	
2	10	27	
3		28	
4		29	
5		30	
6		31	
7		32	
8	1000	33	100001
9		34	
10		35	
11		36	
12		37	
13		38	
14		39	
15		40	
16		41	
17	10001	42	
18		43	
19		44	
20		45	
21		46	
22		47	
23		48	
24		49	
25		50	110010

Base Two Table Answer Key
(Teacher Resource 1)

Directions: Write these Base Ten numerals in Base Two notation. Some examples have been provided for you.

Base Ten Numerals	Base Two Numerals	Base Ten Numerals	Base Two Numerals
1	1	26	11010
2	10	27	11011
3	11	28	11100
4	100	29	11101
5	101	30	11110
6	110	31	11111
7	111	32	100000
8	1000	33	100001
9	1001	34	100010
10	1010	35	100011
11	1011	36	100100
12	1100	37	100101
13	1101	38	100110
14	1110	39	100111
15	1111	40	101000
16	10000	41	101001
17	10001	42	101010
18	10010	43	101011
19	10011	44	101100
20	10100	45	101101
21	10101	46	101110
22	10110	47	101111
23	10111	48	110000
24	11000	49	110001
25	11001	50	110010

Base Two Problems (Handout 6C)

Directions: Complete the following problems and show your work.

1. $11001_{\text{Base Two}}$ = _____ Base Ten

2. $100001_{\text{Base Two}}$ = _____ Base Ten

3. $43_{\text{Base Ten}}$ = _____ Base Two

4. $78_{\text{Base Ten}}$ = _____ Base Two

Base Two Problems Answer Key (Teacher Resource 2)

Directions: Complete the following problems and show your work.

1. $11001_{\text{Base Two}} =$ _____ Base Ten

$$(1 \times 16) + (1 \times 8) + (0 \times 4) + (0 \times 2) + (1 \times 1) = 16 + 8 + 1 = 25$$

2. $100001_{\text{Base Two}} =$ _____ Base Ten

$$(1 \times 32) + (1 \times 1) = 33$$

3. $43_{\text{Base Ten}} =$ _____ Base Two

101011

4. $78_{\text{Base Ten}} =$ _____ Base Two

1001110

Birthday Trick (Teacher Resource 3)

Directions: Copy the numbers below onto five large pieces of sturdy cardboard (file folders work well), and use a thick marker. Have a student think about the *day* of the month on which he or she was born. For example, if it is March 14, she thinks about 14. Have the student point to the cards that contain his or her number. In this case, the student would say Cards B, C, and D. You can guess his or her number by adding the first number in each column that she indicated (2 + 4 + 8).

Card A	Card B	Card C	Card D	Card E
1	2	4	8	16
3	3	5	9	17
5	6	6	10	18
7	7	7	11	19
9	10	12	12	20
11	11	13	13	21
13	14	14	14	22
15	15	15	15	23
17	18	20	24	24
19	19	21	25	25
21	22	22	26	26
23	23	23	27	27
25	26	28	28	28
27	27	29	29	29
29	30	30	30	30
31	31	31	31	31

Note to teacher: This is the table that explains which of the numbers 1–31 belong on which cards for the Birthday Guessing Trick. (Note that these are the first 31 answers to Handout 6B.)

Base Ten	Sixteens or 2^4	Eights or 2^3	Fours or 2^2	Twos or 2^1	Units or 2^0
1					1
2				1	0
3				1	1
4			1	0	0
5			1	0	1
6			1	1	0
7			1	1	1
8		1	0	0	0
9		1	0	0	1
10		1	0	1	0
11		1	0	1	1
12		1	1	0	0
13		1	1	0	1
14		1	1	1	0
15		1	1	1	1
16	1	0	0	0	0
17	1	0	0	0	1
18	1	0	0	1	0
19	1	0	0	1	1
20	1	0	1	0	0
21	1	0	1	0	1
22	1	0	1	1	0
23	1	0	1	1	1
24	1	1	0	0	0
25	1	1	0	0	1
26	1	1	0	1	0
27	1	1	0	1	1
28	1	1	1	0	0
29	1	1	1	0	1
30	1	1	1	1	0
31	1	1	1	1	1
	Every number that has a 1 in this column goes on card A.	Every number that has a 1 in this column goes on card B.	Every number that has a 1 in this column goes on card C.	Every number that has a 1 in this column goes on card D.	Every number that has a 1 in this column goes on card E.

Extending the Base Two Table to Fractional Parts (Handout 6D)

Directions: Complete the following problems and show your work.

1. Extend the Base Two table to include fractional parts.

4's	2's	1's			

2. Write in expanded notation and then in Base Ten.

   a. $101.11_{\text{Base Two}} = (1 \times 4) + (0 \times 2) + (1 \times 1) + (1 \times \frac{1}{2}) + (1 \times \frac{1}{4}) =$
   $4 + 1 + \frac{1}{2} + \frac{1}{4} = 5\,\frac{3}{4}$ **or 5.75** $_{\text{Base Ten}}$

   b. $11.001 =$

   c. $111.101 =$

Extending the Base Two Table Answer Key (Teacher Resource 4)

1. Extend the Base Two table to include fractional parts.

4's	2's	1's	½'s	¼'s	⅛'s

1. Write in expanded notation and then in Base Ten.

a. $101.11_{\text{Base Two}} = (1 \times 4) + (0 \times 2) + (1 \times 1) + (1 \times ½) + (1 \times ¼) =$
    $4 + 1 + ½ + ¼ = \mathbf{5\ ¾\ or\ 5.75}_{\text{Base Ten}}$

b. $11.001 = (1 \times 2) + (1 \times 1) + (0 \times ½) + (0 \times ¼) + (1 \times ⅛) = 2 + 1 + ⅛ =$
    $\mathbf{3\ ⅛\ or\ 3.125}_{\text{Base Ten}}$

c. $111.101 = (1 \times 4) + (1 \times 2) + (1 \times 1) + (1 \times ½) + (0 \times ¼) + (1 \times ⅛) =$
    $4 + 2 + 1 + ½ + ⅛ = \mathbf{7\ ⅝\ or\ 7.625}_{\text{Base Ten}}$

Extra for Experts! (Handout 6E)

Directions: Can you perform operations in Base Two? Try these problems and then convert the numbers to Base Ten to solve and check. An example is done for you.

Base Two Version of the Problem	Change to Base Ten
1. 　11 +11 110	Check: 　3 +3 　6 Because 110 _{Base Two} = 6 _{Base Ten}, it is likely that the answer in the first column is correct.
2. 　111 +110	
3. Subtract. Remember, this is Base Two! 110 −11	
4. 10111 −1101	
5. Multiply. Remember to regroup every time you have a group of two. 　11 ×11	

Extra for Experts! Answer Key
(Teacher Resource 5)

Directions: Can you perform operations in Base Two? Try these problems and then convert the numbers to Base Ten to solve and check. An example is done for you.

Base Two Version of the Problem	Change to Base Ten

1.
 	
  11
+11
110
	Check:
	  3
	+3
	 6
	
	Because 110 $_{Base\ Two}$ = 6 $_{Base\ Ten}$, it is likely that the answer in the first column is correct.

2. 111 +110 1101	7 +6 13 Because 1101 $_{Base\ Two}$ = 13 $_{Base\ Ten}$, it is likely that the answer in the first column is correct.
3. Subtract. Remember, this is Base Two. 110 −11 11 You can check by addition, too: 11 + 11 = 110	6 −3 3 Because 11 $_{Base\ Two}$ = 3 $_{Base\ Ten}$, it is likely that the answer in the first column is correct.
4. 10111 −1101 1010 Check by adding: 1010 + 1101= 10111	23 −13 10 Because 1010 $_{Base\ Two}$ = 10 $_{Base\ Ten}$, it is likely that the answer in the first column is correct.
5. Multiply. Remember to regroup every time you have a group of two. 11 ×11 11 110 1001	3 ×3 9 Because 1001 $_{Base\ Two}$ = 9 $_{Base\ Ten}$, it is likely that the answer in the first column is correct.

Lesson 7: Mayans and Base Twenty

Instructional Purpose

- To learn about the Base Twenty and the Mayan number system

Materials and Handouts

- Mayan Symbol Chart (Handout 7A)
- Place Value Table (Handout 7B)
- Mayan Practice (Handout 7C)
- Mayan Practice Answer Key (Teacher Resource 1)
- Mayan Table (Handout 7D)
- Mayan Table Answer Key (Teacher Resource 2)

Activities

1. Display the **Mayan Symbol Chart (Handout 7A)** on the overhead projector and give students their own copies. Explain that this is the symbol chart for the number system used by the Mayan people who lived in the Yucatan peninsula of Mexico about 3,000 years ago. Have them list all of the observations about it that they can. Make sure students recognize the following key points.
   - There are 20 symbols.
   - They had a symbol that was used as a placeholder, similar to our zero.
   - The Mayan symbols are similar to a Base Five system.

2. Distribute the **Place Value Table (Handout 7B)** and tell students that they do not have to generate the table for the Mayan system on their own because it has a strange twist. Examine the table as a class and discuss how it is different.

3. Explain that the Mayans, as well as the Babylonians, loved the number 360 and they created a number system to use this number. They designed a modified place value system where every place after the two on the right has a factor of 360. The Mayan people did not use fractions. Their interest in Base Twenty probably came from counting their fingers and toes. Beyond that, their main interest in counting was astronomy and calendars. Like the Babylonians, they knew how many days there were in a year, but preferred the 360-day year. They used 18 months of 20 days each and 5 holidays as a bonus at the end.

4. Tell students that the Mayans recorded their numbers vertically and this is represented on the bottom of the Place Value Table handout.

5. Distribute **Mayan Practice (Handout 7C)** in order to demonstrate the vertical arrangement used by the Mayans. The larger place values are listed above the smaller place values. Have students interpret the value of the numbers given by using the Mayan Symbol Chart.

6. Distribute the **Mayan Table (Handout 7D)** and have students work in groups to complete it.

Math Journal

- Discuss the similarities and differences between the Babylonian number system and the Mayan number system. Why do you think that these two systems did not continue into present-day civilizations?

Assessment

- Mayan Table (Handout 7D)

Note to Teacher

Students may find the presence of the single factor of 18 in the place value chart too distracting. If so, do not be discouraged from using this lesson, because the use of the symbol for zero is a *big* idea. Also, the historical aspects of how number systems in different parts of the world developed are worth investigating. It is better to expose students to this lesson with extra support from you than not to attempt it.

Extensions

The following student activities can be used to extend the lesson.
1. Base Twenty is called a vigesimal system. Look up *vigesimal* in a dictionary and find the origin of the word.

2. Compare and contrast the number symbols used by the Mayans and the symbols used by the Babylonians. Which symbols do you think are easier to recognize and use?

3. Find out why the Mayans used the clamshell as their symbol for 0.

Mayan Symbol Chart (Handout 7A)

0	1	2	3	4

5	6	7	8	9

10	11	12	13	14

15	16	17	18	19

Place Value Table (Handout 7B)

18 × 20³	18 × 20²	18 × 20¹	(20¹)	Units (20⁰)

18 × 8,000	
18 × 400	
18 × 20	
20	
Units	

Mayan Practice (Handout 7C)

Directions: Convert the Mayan numerals to numerals in our system.

1.

Answer: _____

2.

Answer: _____

3.

Answer: _____

Mayan Practice Answer Key (Teacher Resource 1)

Directions: Convert the Mayan numerals to numerals in our system.

1.

Answer: $(8 \times 20) + (11 \times 1) = 171$ _{Base Ten}

2.

Answer: $(6 \times 20) + (9 \times 1) = 129$ _{Base Ten}

3.

Answer: $(3 \times 360) + (0 \times 20) + (14 \times 1) = 1,094$ _{Base Ten}

Mayan Table (Handout 7D)

Directions: Write each of these Mayan Base Twenty numbers using the notation of Hindu-Arabic numerals (our customary system) and then give the value in Base Ten.

Mayan	Base Twenty (Using Hindu-Arabic Notation)	Base Ten Value
• • • ——— • ———	8, 11	$(8 \times 20) + (11 \times 1) = 171$
——— ——— ——— • • • •		
	4, 13	
		350
• • • ——— ⟨⟩		
	2, 0, 5	
		483 Hint: $483 = (1 \times 360) + (6 \times 20) + (3 \times 1)$

Mayan Table Answer Key
(Teacher Resource 2)

Directions: Write each of these Mayan Base Twenty numbers using the notation of Hindu-Arabic numerals (our customary system) and then give the value in Base Ten.

Mayan	Base Twenty (Using Hindu-Arabic Notation)	Base Ten Value
• • • — • ═	8, 11	$(8 \times 20) + (11 \times 1) = 171$
═══ ═══ ═══ • • • •	15, 4	$(15 \times 20) + (4 \times 1) = 304$
• • • • • • • ═══	4, 13	$(4 \times 20) + (13 \times 1) = 93$
• • ═══ ═══ ═══	17, 10	$(17 \times 20) + (10 \times 1) = 350$
• • • (shell)	8, 0	$(8 \times 20) + (0 \times 1) = 160$
• • (shell) —	2, 0, 5	$(2 \times 360) + (0 \times 20) + (5 \times 1) = 725$
• • — • • •	1, 6, 3	483 Hint: $483 = (1 \times 360) + (6 \times 20) + (3 \times 1)$

Lesson 8: Changing Bases

Instructional Purpose

- To change a numeral from one number base to another number base when neither expression is Base Ten
- To determine whether a number in any number base is odd or even

Materials and Handouts

- Bases Challenge (Handout 8A)
- Bases Challenge Answer Key (Teacher Resource 1)
- Even or Odd? (Handout 8B)
- Even or Odd? Answer Key (Teacher Resource 2)
- Math manipulatives

Activities

1. Use the following questions to ensure student understanding of odds, evens, and their sums before beginning the lesson activities.
   - What does it mean to say a number is even? (When you divide by two, there is no remainder.)
   - What does it mean to say that a number is odd? (When you divide by two, there is a remainder of one.)
   - What can you say about the sum of two odd numbers? (The sum is even.)
   - What can you say about the sum of two even numbers? (The sum is even.)
   - What can you say about the sum of an odd number and an even number? (The sum is odd.)
   - How do you tell if a multidigit number is odd or even in Base Ten? (Look at the units digit and if it is odd, the whole number is odd. If it is even, the whole number is even.)
   - Why does this rule work? (Every digit to the left of the units' digit is a multiple of 10, so it is even. If you write the number in expanded notation such as $345 = [(3 \times 100) + (4 \times 10) + (5 \times 1)]$, this suggests you are adding even + even + odd. The state of the units digit determines whether the entire sum is even or odd.)

2. Distribute **Bases Challenge (Handout 8A)** and have students work in groups to solve the first problem. Discuss their results and strategies. Have manipulatives available if students need them and tell students to complete the rest of the challenge problems.

3. Have students work in groups to create three original problems similar to those in the Bases Challenge and an answer key. Encourage groups to exchange problems and grade each other's work.

4. Distribute **Even or Odd? (Handout 8B)** and have students work in groups to complete it. Discuss the answers as a whole class.

5. Ask the following questions one at a time. Have students discuss them in groups and then have groups report their solutions. Encourage students to use math problem-solving strategies such as guess and check. Have math manipulatives available for student use.

Can each of these happen if A and B are different whole numbers? If so, find A and B.

- $123_{\text{Base A}} = 123_{\text{Base B}}$ (No. If the bases are different the values of each column are different and the two expressions would not be equal.)
- $1{,}013_{\text{Base A}} = 3{,}201_{\text{Base B}}$ (A = 6 and B = 4)
- $52_{\text{Base B}}$ is twice as big as $25_{\text{Base B}}$ (B = 8)

Math Journal

Sometimes items are packaged and sold in the following ways:

1 dozen = 12
1 gross = 144
1 great gross = 1,768

- What number base does this system use?
- What kinds of things might be packaged this way?
- Do you think it is any better than Base Ten for packaging? Explain.

Assessment

- Bases Challenge (Handout 8A)
- Even or Odd? (Handout 8B)
- Math journal assignment

Extensions

The following student activities can be used to extend the lesson.

1. Write your age in Base Two, Base Three, Base Four, Base Five, Base Six, Base Seven, Base Eight, Base Nine, Base Ten, and Base Twenty. Which is the longest? Which is the shortest?

2. Learn how to use a Chinese abacus to show the numbers 1 through 20. Does the abacus use place value? Make a presentation to the class to show how to add using an abacus.

3. Write a program for a graphing calculator to change a number in one base to another.

4. See http://www.cut-the-knot.org/binary.shtml for a Web site that converts numbers from one number base to another.

5. Palindromic numbers (palindromes) are the same when written forward or backward. Use a highlighter to mark the palindromic numbers in your Base Two chart. Do you think palindromes are more common in Base Two or Base Ten numerals? Why?

6. Make a general statement about how to recognize evens and odds in Base Three.

Bases Challenge (Handout 8A)

Directions: Find the number that belongs in the blank. Show your work.

1. $24_{\text{Base Five}} =$ _____ Base Two

2. $57_{\text{Base Ten}} =$ _____ Base Two

3. $243_{\text{Base Six}} =$ _____ Base Ten

4. $125_{\text{Base Six}} =$ _____ Base Two

5. $231_{\text{Base Four}} =$ _____ Base Ten

6. $125_{\text{Base Eight}} =$ _____ Base Five

7.   Write an explanation of how you solved Problem 6.

_____

_____

_____

_____

_____

Bases Challenge Answer Key
(Teacher Resource 1)

Directions: Find the number that belongs in the blank. Show your work.

1. $24_{\text{Base Five}} = \underline{\textbf{1110}}_{\text{Base Two}}$

2. $57_{\text{Base Ten}} = \underline{\textbf{111001}}_{\text{Base Two}}$

3. $243_{\text{Base Six}} = \underline{\textbf{99}}_{\text{Base Ten}}$

4. $125_{\text{Base Six}} = \underline{\textbf{110101}}_{\text{Base Two}}$

5. $231_{\text{Base Four}} = \underline{\textbf{45}}_{\text{Base Ten}}$

6. $125_{\text{Base Eight}} = \underline{\textbf{320}}_{\text{Base Five}}$

7.   Write an explanation of how you solved Problem 6.

   Make a Base Eight place value table to show what the value of each digit is. The 1 is 1 group of 64, the 2 is 2 groups of 8, and the 5 is 5 groups of 1. So $(1 \times 64) + (2 \times 8) + (5 \times 1) = 64 + 16 + 5 = 85$ in Base Ten. Then, separate 85 into groups that fit into the Base Five place value table: 3 groups of 25, 2 groups of 5, and no ones. That makes 320 in Base Five.

Even or Odd? (Handout 8B)

Directions: Decide if each number is even or odd. Show your work.

1. 1,111 _{Base Two}

2. 1,111 _{Base Three}

3. 1,111 _{Base Four}

4. 1,212 _{Base Three}

5. Make a general statement about how to recognize evens and odds in Base Four. What other bases follow this rule?

   _____

   _____

   _____

6. Without converting to Base Ten, decide if each of the following is odd or even. Show your work.

   a. 3,333 _{Base Four}

   b. 1,111 _{Base Five}

   c. 1,111 _{Base Six}

   d. 1,234 _{Base Five}

Even or Odd? Answer Key
(Teacher Resource 2)

Directions: Decide if each number is even or odd. Show your work.

1. $1,111_{\text{Base Two}}$

    Odd; $(1 \times 8) + (1 \times 4) + (1 \times 2) + (1 \times 1)$ suggests that even + even + even + odd = odd

2. $1,111_{\text{Base Three}}$

    Even; $(1 \times 27) + (1 \times 9) + (1 \times 3) + (1 \times 1)$ suggests that odd + odd + odd + odd = even

3. $1,111_{\text{Base Four}}$

    Odd; $(1 \times 64) + (1 \times 16) + (1 \times 8) + (1 \times 1)$ suggests that even + even + even + odd = odd

4. $1,212_{\text{Base Three}}$

    Odd; $(2 \times 27) + (2 \times 9) + (1 \times 3) + (2 \times 1)$ suggests that even + even + odd + even = odd

5.   Make a general statement about how to recognize evens and odds in Base Four. What other bases follow this rule?

    All columns to the left of the units are multiples of 4, so they are even. Therefore, the parity (odd/even) is determined by the units column. It is really the same rule that is used in Base Ten. Any even base also follows this rule.

6.   Without converting to Base Ten, decide if each of the following is odd or even. Show your work.

    a. $3,333_{\text{Base Four}}$

        Odd; Apply your rule from #5 or note that $(3 \times 64) + (3 \times 16) + (3 \times 8) + (13 \times 1)$ suggests that even + even + even + odd = odd

    b. $1,111_{\text{Base Five}}$

        Even; $(1 \times 125) + (1 \times 25) + (1 \times 5) + (1 \times 1)$ suggests that odd + odd + odd + odd = even

c. 1,111 _{Base Six}

Odd; (1 × 216) + (1 × 36) + (1 × 6) + (1 × 1) suggests that even + even + even + odd = odd

d. 1,234 _{Base Five}

Even; (1 × 125) + (2 × 25) + (3 × 5) + (4 × 1) suggests that odd + even + odd + even = even

Lesson 9: Operations in Various Bases

Instructional Purpose

- To perform the four basic operations in number bases other than Base Ten

Materials and Handouts

- Tables in Base Five (Handout 9A)
- Tables in Base Five Answer Key (Teacher Resource 1)
- Addition (Handout 9B)
- Addition Answer Key (Teacher Resource 2)
- Operation Challenge (Handout 9C)
- Operation Challenge Answer Key (Teacher Resource 3)
- Binary Operations (Handout 9D)
- Binary Operations Answer Key (Teacher Resource 4)
- Time Operations (Handout 9E)
- Time Operations Answer Key (Teacher Resource 5)

Activities

1. Ask students to make a multiplication "table" in Base Ten for numbers 1–5 as an example of a number fact table. It should look similar to the one below.

×	1	2	3	4	5
1	1	2	3	4	5
2	2	4	6	8	10
3	3	6	9	12	15
4	4	8	12	16	20
5	5	10	15	20	25

2. Distribute the **Tables in Base Five (Handout 9A)** and suggest that the students on Planet Evifesab need to learn their basic addition and multiplication facts. Have students complete the tables and discuss as a class.

3. Challenge students to think about Base Seven. If you add in Base Seven, you need to regroup each time you have a group of seven. Have students try the following problem and discuss as a class.

$$456_{\text{Base Seven}} + 234_{\text{Base Seven}} = ? \ (1023_{\text{Base Seven}})$$

4. Let students work in groups to complete **Addition (Handout 9B)** for practice computing in various number bases. Debrief as a class.

5. Have students work in groups to try to multiply 24×3 in Base Five and then have them present and justify their answers. They may use the Base Five multiplication tables they completed in Handout 9A. (The usual multiplication algorithm applies here, but when each group of five is reached, there is a regrouping.)

24 Base Five $\times 3$ Base Five	34 Base Five $\times 23$ Base Five
Using partial products: 24 Base Five $\times 3$ Base Five 22 $(3 \times 4 = 22_{\text{Base Five}})$ 110 $(3 \times 20 = 3 \times 10_{\text{Base Ten}} = 110_{\text{Base Five}})$ 132 (To check, you may change the factors into Base Ten, multiply, and convert the answer back to Base Five.)	Answer, using partial products within Base Five: 34 Base Five $\times 23$ Base Five 22 (3×4) 140 (3×30) 130 (20×4) 1100 (20×30) 1442

6. Continue in the same fashion with these subtraction problems in Base Four. Note that when you regroup from the column to the left, you are borrowing a group of 4, not 10.

a.

$$\begin{array}{r} 210 \text{ Base Four} \\ -132 \text{ Base Four} \\ \hline 12 \text{ Base Four} \end{array}$$

b.

$$\begin{array}{r} 321 \text{ Base Four} \\ -123 \text{ Base Four} \\ \hline 132 \text{ Base Four} \end{array}$$

7. Divide students into groups and have them work on one of the following handouts. Discuss as a class their results and thinking.
   - Operation Challenge (Handout 9C)
   - Binary Numbers (Handout 9D)
   - Time Operations (Handout 9E; this is the least challenging of the three handouts).

8. Give students an additional challenge problem. Tell students that you are on a mission to another galaxy. You land your starship on a planet where you observe the following notation written on a cliff:

$$13 + 15 = 31$$
$$10 \times 10 = 100$$
$$6 \times 3 = 24$$

If you assume that the local inhabitants developed their counting system using a number base that is the number of fingers they have, figure out how many fingers they might have. Explain how you know.

81

(They have seven fingers. You know there must be more than six because the digit 6 is used in the notation. By trial and error, you find that Base Seven makes all three statements true. If you know some algebra, you can generate the following from the third statement: write the equation $6 \times 3 = 2x + 4$ [where x is the place value of the 2]. In Base Ten, $6 \times 3 = 18$ so this means $18 = 2x + 4$. Solve it and you get $x = 7$.)

Assessment

- Tables in Base Five (Handout 9A)
- Addition (Handout 9B)
- Operation Challenge (Handout 9C)
- Binary Operations (Handout 9D)
- Time Operations (Handout 9E)

Notes to Teacher

1. There are examples in this lesson that use bases other than Base Ten. Base Five and Base Two are featured in the unit. Your strongest students should be able to make the transition to Base Six or Base Eight or any other base. Use your judgment about what to require or make the new bases optional or an extra challenge problem.

2. Division is the toughest of the operations in other number bases. You might ask students to verify the answers in the key for the division problems included here by using multiplication if it is too difficult to find the answers on their own.

3. One way students can check their computations is to convert each Base X number into Base Ten, do the computation in Base Ten, and convert the answer back to Base X. Do not tell students this strategy, but push them in the debriefing of the first couple of problems. This is an example of a very common strategy in mathematical problem solving: change the problem into one you know how to solve, solve it, and then change the answer to the original form. Do not let students use this as their only strategy; they should stay within the given number base and try the usual algorithm within that base. This will challenge their understanding of the algorithms and place value in Base Ten.

Extensions

The following student activities can be used to extend the lesson.

1. Create your own problems using different operations in various number bases. Exchange with other group members to solve them. Save the problems on cards and create a file.

2. Create operations tables for addition and multiplication in Base Six.

Tables in Base Five (Handout 9A)

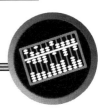

Directions: Enter the sum of each pair of digits in Base Five.

+	0	1	2	3	4
0					
1					
2				**10**	
3					
4					

Directions: Enter the product of each pair of digits in Base Five.

×	0	1	2	3	4
0					
1					
2				**11**	
3					
4					

Tables in Base Five Answer Key
(Teacher Resource 1)

Directions: Enter the sum of each pair of digits in Base Five.

+	0	1	2	3	4
0	0	1	2	3	4
1	1	2	3	4	10
2	2	3	4	10	11
3	3	4	10	11	12
4	4	10	11	12	13

Directions: Enter the product of each pair of digits in Base Five.

×	0	1	2	3	4
0	0	0	0	0	0
1	0	1	2	3	4
2	0	2	4	11	13
3	0	3	11	14	22
4	0	4	13	22	31

Name_____   Date_____

Addition (Handout 9B)

Directions: Add the following problems in the different bases.

Base Three	Base Seven	Base Six	Base Nine
122 +221	624 +361	425 +323	628 +527

Base Five	Base Two	Base Eight	Base Four
423 +323	111 +101	436 +254	123 +213

Addition Answer Key
(Teacher Resource 2)

Directions: Add the following problems in the different bases.

Base Three	Base Seven	Base Six	Base Nine
122	624	425	628
+221	+361	+323	+527
1120	**1315**	**1152**	**1256**

Base Five	Base Two	Base Eight	Base Four
423	111	436	123
+323	+101	+254	+213
1301	**1100**	**712**	**1002**

Operation Challenge (Handout 9C)

Directions: All of these are Base Five numerals. Complete each of the problems.

1. Multiplication

$$123 \text{ }_{\text{Base Five}}$$
$$\times 24 \text{ }_{\text{Base Five}}$$

2. Addition

$$4211 \text{ }_{\text{Base Five}}$$
$$+3441 \text{ }_{\text{Base Five}}$$

3. Subtraction

$$432 \text{ }_{\text{Base Five}}$$
$$-134 \text{ }_{\text{Base Five}}$$

4. Division

$$233 \text{ }_{\text{Base Five}} \div 4 \text{ }_{\text{Base Five}} =$$

5. Division (in Base Five)

$$23\overline{)124}$$

Operation Challenge Answer Key (Teacher Resource 3)

Directions: All of these are Base Five numerals. Complete each of the problems.

1. Multiplication

$$123 \text{ Base Five}$$
$$\times 24 \text{ Base Five}$$

4112

2. Addition

$$4211 \text{ Base Five}$$
$$+3441 \text{ Base Five}$$

13202

3. Subtraction

$$432 \text{ Base Five}$$
$$-134 \text{ Base Five}$$

243

4. Division

$$233 \text{ Base Five} \div 4 \text{ Base Five} =$$

32 Base Five

5. Division (in Base Five)

$$23\overline{)124} \quad \overset{3}{\phantom{23\overline{)124}}}$$

Binary Operations (Handout 9D)

Directions: All of these are Base Two numerals. Complete each of the problems.

1. Multiplication

```
  101
×  11
```

2. Addition

```
 1011
+ 101
```

3. Subtraction

```
 1001
− 111
```

4. Addition

```
 1111
+1011
```

5. Division

$1111 \div 11 =$

Binary Operations Answer Key
(Teacher Resource 4)

Directions: All of these are Base Two numerals. Complete each of the problems.

1. Multiplication

$$
\begin{array}{r}
101 \\
\times 11 \\
\hline
\mathbf{101} \\
\underline{\mathbf{1010}} \\
\mathbf{1111}
\end{array}
$$

2. Addition

$$
\begin{array}{r}
1011 \\
+101 \\
\hline
\mathbf{10000}
\end{array}
$$

3. Subtraction

$$
\begin{array}{r}
1001 \\
-111 \\
\hline
\mathbf{10}
\end{array}
$$

4. Addition

$$
\begin{array}{r}
1111 \\
+1011 \\
\hline
\mathbf{11010}
\end{array}
$$

5. Division

$1111 \div 11 = \mathbf{101}$

Time Operations (Handout 9E)

Directions: Complete these computations.

1.

       3 hrs, 24 minutes, 20 seconds
  + 1 hr, 10 minutes, 41 seconds
  <u>   </u>

2.

       4 hrs, 45 minutes, 30 seconds
  + 5 hrs, 20 minutes, 46 seconds
  <u>   </u>

3.

  10 hrs, 55 minutes, 10 seconds
  + 2 hr, 20 minutes, 30 seconds
  <u>   </u>

4.

  2 hrs, 25 minutes, 20 seconds
  –   5 minutes, 40 seconds
  <u>   </u>

5.

  12 hrs, 25 minutes, 50 seconds
  – 4 hrs, 35 minutes, 55 seconds
  <u>   </u>

6.

  22 hrs, 21 minutes, 15 seconds
  – 5 hrs, 36 minutes, 30 seconds
  <u>   </u>

Time Operations Answer Key
(Teacher Resource 5)

Directions: Complete these computations.

1.

      3 hrs, 24 minutes, 20 seconds
    + 1 hr, 10 minutes, 41 seconds
        4 hr, 35 minutes, 1 second

2.

      4 hrs, 45 minutes, 30 seconds
    + 5 hrs, 20 minutes, 46 seconds
     10 hrs, 6 minutes, 16 seconds

3.

    10 hrs, 55 minutes, 10 seconds
  + 2 hr, 20 minutes, 30 seconds
   13 hrs, 15 minutes, 40 seconds

4.

    2 hrs, 25 minutes, 20 seconds
  −   5 minutes, 40 seconds
    2 hr, 19 minutes, 40 seconds

5.

   12 hrs, 25 minutes, 50 seconds
  − 4 hrs, 35 minutes, 55 seconds
    7 hrs, 49 minutes, 55 seconds

6.

   22 hrs, 21 minutes, 15 seconds
  − 5 hrs, 36 minutes, 30 seconds
   16 hrs, 44 minutes, 45 seconds

Lesson 10: Postassessment

Instructional Purpose
- To review the major concepts of the unit
- To administer the postassessment for the unit

Materials and Handouts
- Postassessment (Handout 10A)
- Postassessment Answer Key (Teacher Resource 1)

Activities
1. Congratulate students on their success with the unit. Have them share what they learned from their favorite activities.

2. Distribute the **Postassessment (Handout 10A)** and have students complete it individually. Collect and score the assessments using the **Postassessment Answer Key (Teacher Resource 1)**.

3. Have students compare their preassessment to their postassessment responses. Ask them to write in their journals about what they have learned and how they have grown as mathematicians throughout the course of the unit.

Note to Teacher
The postassessment is parallel in structure to the preassessment for this unit. Change any sets of questions to mirror any changes you made in the preassessment.

Postassessment (Handout 10A)

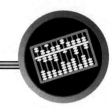

Directions: Do your best to answer the following questions.

1. What is the value of the digit **8** in each of these Base Ten numerals?

    a. 8,274 _____

    b. 204.386 _____

2. What is the value of the digit **2** in each of these Base Five numerals?

    a. 1,243 _{Base Five} _____

    b. 3.21 _{Base Five} _____

3. Write 746 in Roman numerals. _____

4. What is the difference between the meanings of the terms *number* and *numeral*? Give examples.

5. $321_{\text{Base Five}} = \underline{\hspace{2cm}}_{\text{Base Ten}}$

6. $25_{\text{Base Ten}} = \underline{\hspace{2cm}}_{\text{Base Two}}$

7. $2{,}002_{\text{Base Three}} = \underline{\hspace{2cm}}_{\text{Base Seven}}$

8. Suppose that archaeologists find that the inhabitants of an old city called Trugo wrote some of their numbers in this way:

Our system	1	2	3	4	5	6	7	8	9	10	20	30	40	50	60	70	80	90	100
Trugo's system	A	B	C	D	E	F	G	H	I	a	b	c	d	e	f	g	h	i	Z

The number we write as **37** would be written as **cG** in the Trugo system. Does the Trugo system use place value? How do you know?

9. Add these two numbers that are written in Base Six notation.

$\begin{array}{r} 223_{\text{ Base Six}} \\ +453_{\text{ Base Six}} \\ \hline _{\text{ Base Six}} \end{array}$

10. How many symbols are needed to form a Base Twenty number system? _____
Explain your reasoning.

11. Complete the headings for this Base Sixty place value table. The units column has been done for you.

		Ones (units)

Postassessment Answer Key
(Teacher Resource 1)

Directions: Do your best to answer the following questions.

1. What is the value of the digit **8** in each of these Base Ten numerals?

   a. 8,274   **8,000 or eight thousand**

   b. 204.386   **8⁄100 or eight hundredths**

2. What is the value of the digit **2** in each of these Base Five numerals?

   a. 1,243 ₍Base Five₎   **50 or 2 × 25 or two twenty-fives**

   b. 3.21 ₍Base Five₎   **2⁄5 or 2 × 1⁄5 or two fifths**

3. Write 746 in Roman numerals.   **DCCXLVI**

4. What is the difference between the meanings of the terms *number* and *numeral*? Give examples.

   Number is the concept of "how many," whereas numeral is the written expression (notation) of the number. There are many ways (numerals) to write a number.

5. $321_{\text{Base Five}} = \underline{\mathbf{86}}_{\text{Base Ten}}$

6. $25_{\text{Base Ten}} = \underline{\mathbf{11001}}_{\text{Base Two}}$

7. $2{,}002_{\text{Base Three}} = \underline{\mathbf{110}}_{\text{Base Seven}}$

8. Suppose that archaeologists find that the inhabitants of an old city called Trugo wrote some of their numbers in this way:

Our system	1	2	3	4	5	6	7	8	9	10	20	30	40	50	60	70	80	90	100
Trugo's system	A	B	C	D	E	F	G	H	I	a	b	c	d	e	f	g	h	i	Z

The number we write as **37** would be written as **cG** in the Trugo system. Does the Trugo system use place value? How do you know?

The Trugo system does not use place value; wherever the symbols move, they keep the same value—it does not depend on placement.

9. Add these two numbers that are written in Base Six notation.

$$223_{\text{Base Six}}$$
$$+453_{\text{Base Six}}$$
$$\overline{1120}_{\text{Base Six}}$$

10. How many symbols are needed to form a Base Twenty number system? <u>20</u>
Explain your reasoning.

You need one symbol for each number from 0–19. When you get a group of 20, you write 10 meaning "one group of twenty and no ones." So, the symbols can be reused by representing higher values when placed in a new position.

11. Complete the headings for this Base Sixty place value table. The units column has been done for you.

3,600's or (60 × 60) or 60^2	60's	Ones (units)

Part III:
Unit Extensions

Unit Extensions

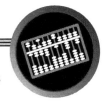

1. Look at the dots in the diagram. Write as many different numerals as you can using different bases to tell how many dots there are.

2. If you could travel back to 4000 BC in a time machine, what recommendation would you make to the Babylonians about what number system they should adopt and why?

3. Choose one of the cultures listed. Find out about the earliest known number system of this culture and report to your classmates.
    *   Egyptian
    *   Hebrew
    *   Greek
    *   Chinese
    *   Indian
    *   Any other culture that interests you

    Answer the following questions about the number system you have chosen:
    *   How did the people of this culture write the numerals for the numbers 1 through 10?
    *   Did the number system use place value? How do you know?
    *   Did the system use a symbol for zero? How do you know?
    *   Think about the numbers that you know as 31 and 125. How can you write them in the numerals of the culture you have chosen?

4. Imagine that you live in the year 200 A.D. and want to create a number system for your civilization.
    *   Create (on a single sheet of paper) evidence of that system for future archaeologists.
    *   Exchange papers and have the other students try to determine how your number system works while you figure out theirs.

5. Arrange the digits 1, 2, 3, 4, 5, 6, 7, 8, and 9 in the boxes below to make a correct addition problem. You may only use each digit once.

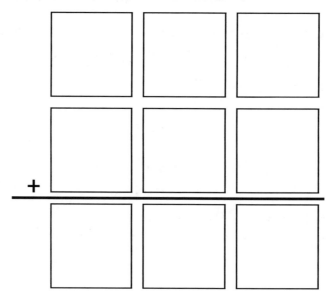

- 219 + 348 = 567 is one solution. Use it to find more. How many solutions can exist that have the sum 567? Explain how place value is important in rearranging the digits of this solution in terms of getting a new one.

- Questions to consider:
    - What is the effect of interchanging two of the columns?
    - Is there any column where the 9 cannot be placed?
    - Will all solutions require regrouping (carrying)?
    - What is the smallest sum that can be made?
    - What is the largest sum that can be made?

- There are more than 300 solutions to the problem. See how many you can find. Determine a way to catalog them so that you know if you have duplicates in your list.

Common Core State Standards Alignment

Lesson	Common Core State Standards in Math
Lesson 1: Preassessment	3.NBT.A Use place value understanding and properties of operations to perform multi-digit arithmetic.
	4.OA.C Generate and analyze patterns.
	4.NBT.A Generalize place value understanding for multi-digit whole numbers.
	5.OA.B Analyze patterns and relationships.
	4.NBT.B Use place value understanding and properties of operations to perform multi-digit arithmetic.
	5.NBT.A Understand the place value system.
Lesson 2: Introduction to Place Value	4.NBT.A Generalize place value understanding for multi-digit whole numbers.
	5.NBT.A Understand the place value system.
Lesson 3: Super Bowl XXXIX	3.OA.D Solve problems involving the four operations, and identify and explain patterns in arithmetic.
	4.OA.C Generate and analyze patterns.
	5.OA.B Analyze patterns and relationships
Lesson 4: Base Five	4.NBT.A Generalize place value understanding for multi-digit whole numbers.
	4.MD.A Solve problems involving measurement and conversion of measurements.
	5.NBT.A Understand the place value system.
	5.MD.A Convert like measurement units within a given measurement system.
Lesson 5: Babylonians and Base Sixty	3.OA.D Solve problems involving the four operations, and identify and explain patterns in arithmetic.
	3.MD.A Solve problems involving measurement and estimation.
	4.OA.B Gain familiarity with factors and multiples.
	4.OA.C Generate and analyze patterns.
	4.NF.C Understand decimal notation for fractions, and compare decimal fractions.
	4.MD.A Solve problems involving measurement and conversion of measurements.
	5.OA.B Analyze patterns and relationships.
	5.NBT.A Understand the place value system.
Lesson 6: Base Two	3.NBT.A Use place value understanding and properties of operations to perform multi-digit arithmetic.
	4.OA.C Generate and analyze patterns.
	4.NBT.A Generalize place value understanding for multi-digit whole numbers.
	4.NF.C Understand decimal notation for fractions, and compare decimal fractions.
	4.MD.A Solve problems involving measurement and conversion of measurements.

Lesson	Common Core State Standards in Math
Lesson 6: Base Two, *continued*	5.OA.B Analyze patterns and relationships.
	5.NBT.A Understand the place value system.
	5.MD.A Convert like measurement units within a given measurement system.
Lesson 7: Mayans and Base Twenty	4.OA.B Gain familiarity with factors and multiples.
	4.OA.C Generate and analyze patterns.
	5.OA.B Analyze patterns and relationships.
	5.NBT.A Understand the place value system.
	6.EE.A Apply and extend previous understandings of arithmetic to algebraic expressions.
Lesson 8: Changing Bases	3.OA.D Solve problems involving the four operations, and identify and explain patterns in arithmetic.
	4.OA.C Generate and analyze patterns.
	4.NBT.A Generalize place value understanding for multi-digit whole numbers.
	4.MD.A Solve problems involving measurement and conversion of measurements.
	5.OA.B Analyze patterns and relationships.
	5.NBT.A Understand the place value system.
	5.MD.A Convert like measurement units within a given measurement system.
Lesson 9: Operations in Various Bases	3.NBT.A Use place value understanding and properties of operations to perform multi-digit arithmetic.
	4.NBT.B Use place value understanding and properties of operations to perform multi-digit arithmetic.
	5.NBT.A Understand the place value system.
	5.NBT.B Perform operations with multi-digit whole numbers and with decimals to hundredths.
Lesson 10: Postassessment	3.NBT.A Use place value understanding and properties of operations to perform multi-digit arithmetic.
	4.OA.C Generate and analyze patterns.
	4.NBT.A Generalize place value understanding for multi-digit whole numbers.
	5.OA.B Analyze patterns and relationships.
	4.NBT.B Use place value understanding and properties of operations to perform multi-digit arithmetic.
	5.NBT.A Understand the place value system.